GROWING UP

Going to Hospital

Vic Parker

www.raintreepublishers.co.uk
Visit our website to find out
more information about
Raintree books.

To order:
☎ Phone 0845 6044371
🖹 Fax +44 (0) 1865 312263
🖳 Email myorders@raintreepublishers.co.uk

Customers from outside the UK please telephone +44 1865 312262

Raintree is an imprint of Capstone Global Library
Limited, a company incorporated in England and Wales
having its registered office at 7 Pilgrim Street, London,
EC4V 6LB – Registered company number: 6695582

Edited by Dan Nunn, Rebecca Rissman, and Sian Smith
Designed by Joanna Hinton-Malivoire
Picture research by Elizabeth Alexander
Originated by Capstone Global Library Ltd
Printed and bound in China by Leo Paper
Products Ltd

ISBN 978 1 406 22046 9 (hardback)
15 14 13 12 11
10 9 8 7 6 5 4 3 2 1

British Library Cataloguing in Publication Data
Parker, Victoria.
  Going to hospital. – (Growing up)
  1. Hospitals–Pictorial works–Juvenile literature.
  2. Therapeutics–Pictorial works–Juvenile literature.
  I. Title II. Series

  362.1'1-dc22

Acknowledgements
We would like to thank the following for permission to
reproduce photographs: Alamy pp. 4 (© Pat Tuson), 5
(© Photofusion Picture Library), 14, 23 glossary patient
(© Blend Images); Corbis pp. 17 (© William Taufic),
18, 23 glossary operation (© Tim Pannell), 19 (©
Rubberball), 21, 23 glossary receptionist (© Deborah
Jaffe); Getty Images pp. 11 (Christopher Furlong), 13, 23
glossary X-ray (Jonatan Fernstrom/Cultura), 16 (Sean
Justice/The Image Bank); iStockphoto p. 8 (© Carmen
Martínez Banús); Photolibrary pp. 7 (SW Productions/
White), 9, 23 glossary ambulance (Image Source), 10
(ERproductions Ltd/Blend Images), 15 (Image100), 20,
23 glossary ward (Jose Luis Pelaez Inc/Blend Images);
Shutterstock pp. 6 (© Monkey Business Images), 12 (©
Andresr), 23 glossary stethoscope (© Adrian Grosu).

Front cover photograph of a boy, a doctor, and a toy
monkey reproduced with permission of Photolibrary
(Laurence Mouton/Photoalto). Back cover photographs
of a stethoscope reproduced with permission of
Shutterstock (© Andresr), and a patient reproduced
with permission of Photolibrary (ERproductions Ltd/
Blend Images).

We would like to thank Jude Taylor and Wendy Arlow for
their invaluable help in the preparation of this book.

Every effort has been made to contact copyright
holders of material reproduced in this book. Any
omissions will be rectified in subsequent printings if
notice is given to the publisher.

Contents

What is a hospital? 4

Why might I go to a hospital?. 6

What is it like being a patient? 8

Who will I meet in hospital? 10

What might happen to me in hospital? 12

How will I feel in hospital? 14

Will I have to stay in hospital?. 16

What will happen if I need an operation?. . . 18

What happens when I leave hospital? 20

How to behave in a hospital 22

Picture glossary 23

Find out more 24

Index 24

Some words are shown in bold, **like this**.
You can find them in the glossary on page 23.

What is a hospital?

A hospital is a building where people go to see a special doctor.

Hospitals are very busy places.

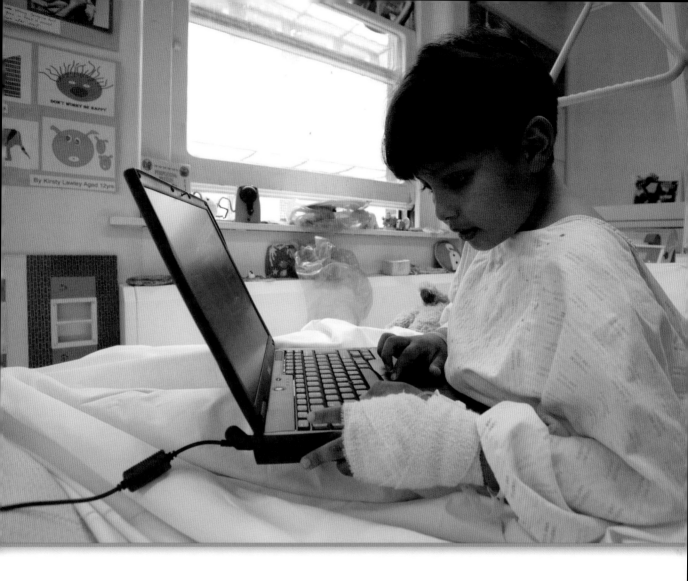

A person who goes to hospital is called a **patient**.

Some patients go in and out of hospital the same day, but others stay for longer.

Why might I go to a hospital?

You might go to hospital to visit a relative or friend who is staying there for a while.

They may have their own room, or be in a **ward** with several other **patients**.

Some patients feel and look much more poorly than others.

You can cheer up a patient by visiting them.

What is it like being a patient?

Sometimes your doctor might ask you to go to hospital as a **patient**.

You can have special tests there to find out if something is wrong with your body.

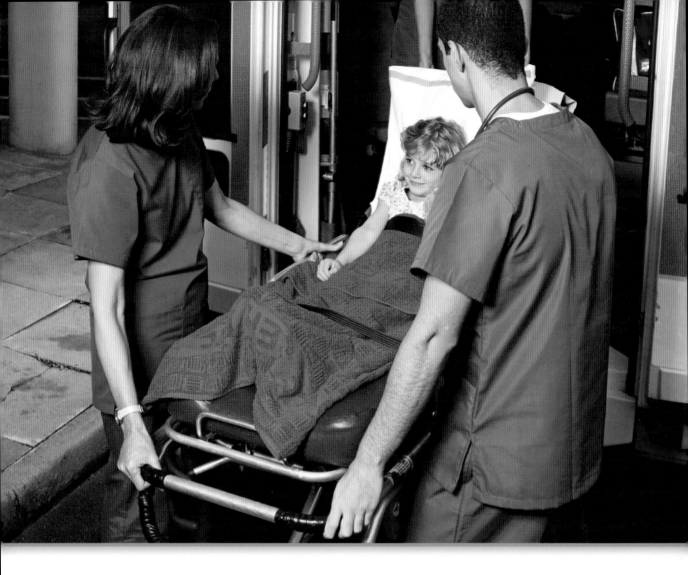

You might also need to go to hospital if you have an accident or are very poorly.

You might go there in an **ambulance**.

Who will I meet in hospital?

There are lots of people who work in a hospital.

If you are a **patient** you will see a doctor or a nurse.

There are lots of other people who work in hospitals, too.

There are **receptionists**, cleaners, play experts, and more.

What might happen to me in hospital?

stethoscope

The doctor or nurse will sometimes ask lots of questions.

They may want to listen to your chest with a **stethoscope**, or take your temperature.

You might go to have special tests done, such as **X-rays**.

An X-ray is a photograph of your bones, so a doctor can see if any are broken.

How will I feel in hospital?

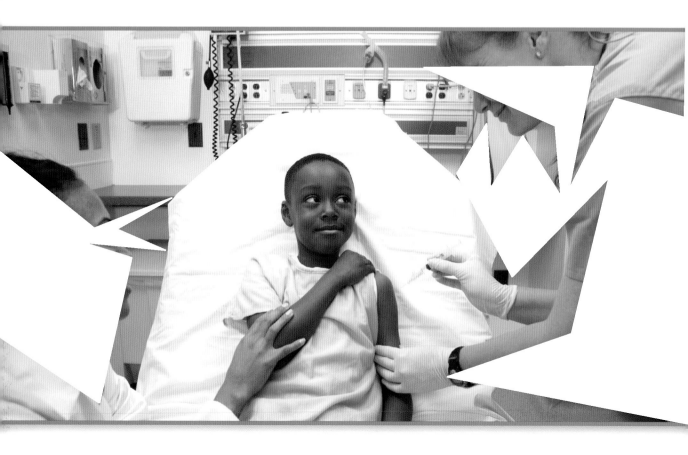

Some medical care might be a bit unpleasant or uncomfortable.

It is natural to be worried sometimes.

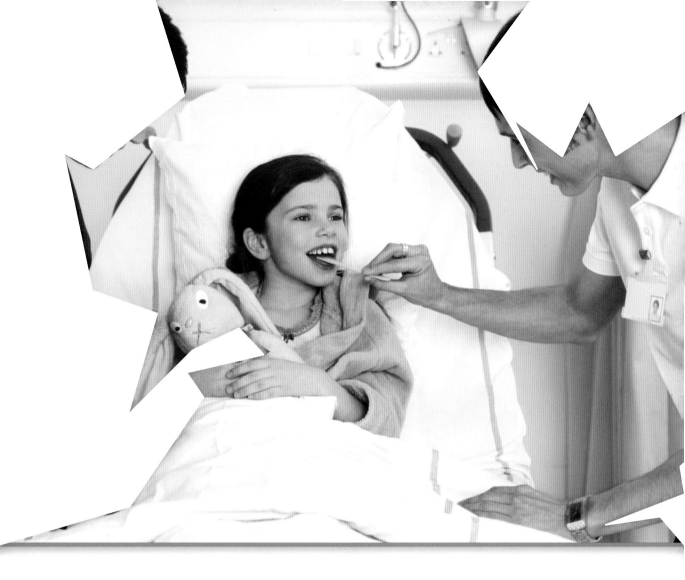

But doctors and nurses are there to look after you.

They do everything because they are trying to help you and make you better.

Will I have to stay in hospital?

Sometimes you have to stay in hospital for a while.

Your mum, dad, or guardian can stay with you.

In the hospital **ward** there will be toys you can play with in bed.

If you do not have to stay in bed, you can go to the ward playroom to play.

What will happen if I need an operation?

An **operation** is when doctors try to fix problems inside your body.

Before the operation, they will give you medicine to make you fall asleep.

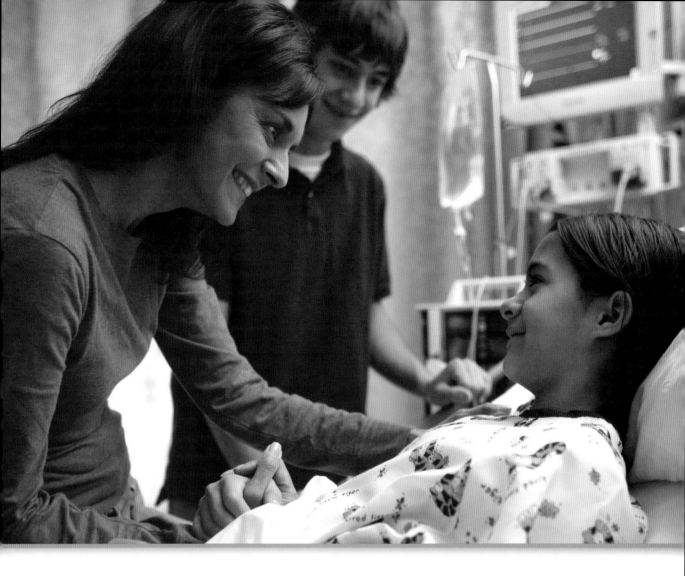

The medicine means you won't feel anything during the operation.

When you wake up, your mum, dad, or guardian will be there with you.

What happens when I leave hospital?

When it is time to leave hospital, you may be given medicine to take with you.

You can take these at home.

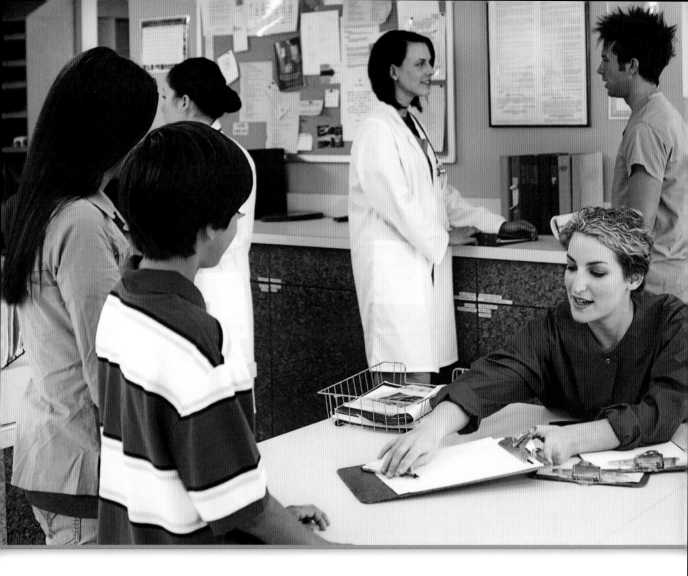

If you need to go back to hospital later, you may be given an appointment.

Then you can come and see a doctor again another day.

How to behave in a hospital

Do:

✓ wash your hands or use hand-cleaning gel to kill any germs

✓ take a **patient** a get well card or a small present such as a magazine.

Don't:

✗ visit a patient if you are poorly – they may catch your illness and become more ill

✗ use a mobile phone. It may disturb people.

Picture glossary

 **ambulance** vehicle that is used to take someone who is very ill to hospital. It has special equipment inside.

 **operation** in an operation, a doctor gives you medicine to put you to sleep while they fix problems inside your body

 **patient** person who goes into hospital to be made better

 **receptionist** person sitting at a desk near the entrance of a building, who meets people and tells them where to go

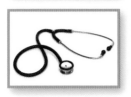 **stethoscope** piece of equipment that a doctor uses to listen to a person's breathing and heartbeat

 **ward** room in a hospital where patients stay until they get better

 **X-ray** photograph of inside the body

Find out more

Books

Do I Have to Go to Hospital?: A First Look at Going to Hospital, Pat Thomas (Wayland, 2008)

My First Visit to Hospital (First Times), Rebecca Hunter (Evans Brothers, 2009)

We Work at the Hospital (Little Nippers), Angela Aylmore (Heinemann Library, 2006)

Websites

Learn more about being in hospital at:
kidshealth.org/kid/

Find out what doctors and nurses can do to help patients at:
www.childrenfirst.nhs.uk

Index

ambulance 9

doctor 4–5, 8, 10, 12–13, 15, 18, 21

medicine 18–19, 20

nurse 10, 12, 15

operation 18–19

patient 5, 6–7, 8, 10, 22

play 17

receptionists 11

stethoscope 12

temperature 12

tests 8

visiting 6–7

ward 6, 17

X-ray 13